Royal Ontario Museum

WARRIOR EMPEROR

中國秦兵馬俑展

AND

CHINA'S

TERRACOTTA

ARMY

CHEN SHEN

Royal Ontario Museum Press

EXHIBITION FLOOR PLAN

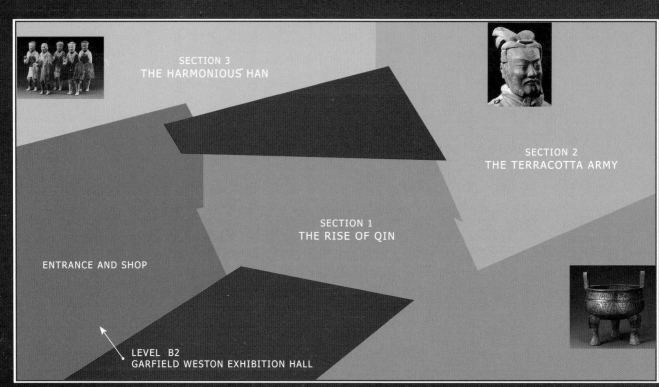

SECTION 3
THE HARMONIOUS HAN

SECTION 2
THE TERRACOTTA ARMY

SECTION 1
THE RISE OF QIN

ENTRANCE AND SHOP

LEVEL B2
GARFIELD WESTON EXHIBITION HALL

CONTENTS

19

Terracotta army Pit No. 1

WELCOME

The fabulous terracotta army of China's First Emperor, Qin Shihuangdi, ranks as one of the world's greatest archaeological finds and one of its most significant cultural treasures. The stuff of legend and lore until its discovery by well diggers in 1974, the life-size figures were interred in an underground tomb complex in China's northern Shaanxi province for more than 2,000 years. It is said that their faces were modelled on those of real, individual warriors—fierce, defiant, compassionate, and noble.

Vigilant in their protection of the emperor in the afterlife, the warriors were accompanied by the accoutrements of eternity, replicas of the emperor's day-to-day material culture, both practical and purely decorative, mirroring his earthly existence: wine vessels, mirrors, jade pendants, stone helmets and armour, bronze daggers, crossbow models, a model of the Xianyang palace, wind chimes, incense burners, female warriors, dancers, acrobats, and much more. Created over several decades,

the army is vast; more than a thousand artisans may have been employed to create the nearly 8,000 sculptures. The Royal Ontario Museum is honoured to have brought a selection of these international treasures to Canada and to have developed an exhibition and associated programming that discuss the nature of ambition, the universally human concept of an afterlife, and the historical roots of modern China. It is the vision of the Museum to bring people together to learn more about the world and in so doing understand more about themselves and each other in an ever-more multicultural societal mosaic.

The ROM is an especially appropriate venue to exhibit China's terracotta warriors. From its earliest days, the Museum has benefitted from astute collectors and generous donors who have helped to build the Museum's Chinese holdings into one of the most important collections outside China. The collection includes a number of the ROM's most iconic objects, among them the mural painting *Paradise of Maitreya* and the tomb mound of the famous General Zu Dashou. The ROM's

Chinese collections are exhibited in four magnificent galleries on the Museum's first floor: the Bishop White Gallery of Chinese Temple Art, the Matthews Family Court of Chinese Sculpture, the Joey and Toby Tanenbaum Gallery of China, and the Gallery of Chinese Architecture, several of which exhibit artifacts from the Zhou, Qin, and Han dynasties featured in *The Warrior Emperor and China's Terracotta Army*. A sampling of ROM artifacts that relate to the exhibition is highlighted in this guide.

The great ROM patron Louise Hawley Stone was passionate about the Asian collections and was the first chair of the ROM's Bishop White Committee, established to support and promote them. Through her leadership the committee grew to be a powerful advocate for the East Asian collections and programs at the Museum, resulting in two endowed curatorial chairs in support of research in China: The Louise Hawley Stone Chair of East Asian Art and The Bishop White Chair of East Asian Art & Archaeology. Dr. Chen Shen, author of this guide and curator of *The*

Warrior Emperor and China's Terracotta Army, is the current, distinguished scholar to hold the prestigious Bishop White Chair. Mrs. Stone's vision and beneficence extended as well to the acquisition of artifacts and specimens and to financial support for ROM research and publications. It is, in fact, because of Mrs. Stone's generosity that the Museum is able to publish this essential guide to the exhibition in a format that is widely accessible—editions are available in English, French, traditional Chinese, and simplified Chinese. We are pleased to be able to provide this value to our visitors—the people of Ontario, Canada, and beyond.

We are also delighted to announce the founding of the Royal Ontario Museum Press, launched with these editions. The Museum has a distinguished history of publishing, characterized by a long list of academic and popular titles, critical acclaim, and awards. This affirmation of the publications program provides a name commensurate with those achievements and with our plans for an even more robust catalogue of works in print and online as we move forward.

We would like to thank the State Administration of Cultural Heritage, People's Republic of China; Shaanxi Provincial Cultural Relics Bureau; and Shaanxi Cultural Heritage Promotion Centre—guardians of the warriors who guarded the First Emperor—for their knowledge and wisdom. The ROM's presentation would not have been possible without the generous support of its presenter, The Robert H. N. Ho Family Foundation; lead sponsor, BMO Financial Group; and supporting sponsor, Cathay Pacific Airways Limited.

Soldiers of destiny, soldiers of eternity, the terracotta warriors of Qin Shihuangdi continue to guard and honour him. In their presence, we cross millennia to witness the power that unified ancient China. We witness as well a record of unbridled ambition.

Like the Great Pyramids, the treasures of Tutankhamun, the Rosetta Stone, and the gold of El Dorado, the terracotta warriors conjure another world.

Dr. Mark D. Engstrom
Deputy Director, Collections and Research

Map of China showing location of the terracotta army

INTRODUCTION

Terracotta warriors

BETWEEN 230 AND 221 BC, the king of the Qin state, Ying Zheng (born 259 BC), conquered six rival states to the east and founded the first united empire—the Qin dynasty (221–206 BC). His actions ended centuries of ongoing warfare and established norms of governance, law, and administration that would characterize China for over 2,000 years.

After unification, Ying Zheng assumed the title *huangdi*, a title never before used in China, to represent his rule over all heaven and earth. He had consolidated the territory his ancestors, dukes of the Qin state, had worked to annex for several hundred years, and he intended his family line to rule the Qin empire for 10,000 generations. Thus, he is known as the First (*shi*) Emperor (*huangdi*) of Qin, or *Qin Shihuangdi*.

Construction of his tomb complex began as soon as he came to the throne at age 13. Nearly 8,000 terracotta warriors were made to guard his underworld empire. The First Emperor could never have dreamed that 2,200 years later, his terracotta soldiers would travel to almost every corner of the world, while he still rests in his mysterious underground palace.

And now his terracotta army has come to Canada.

THE EXHIBITION *The Warrior Emperor and China's Terracotta Army* focuses on the life and afterlife of the First Emperor, showcasing approximately 250 objects loaned from 16 major museums in Shaanxi province in the People's Republic of China. The exhibition is unique to this Canadian tour, as all artifacts have been selected specifically for the four participating Canadian museums. Many have never before been displayed outside China, and some have not previously been displayed in any museum, even in China (see pages 29, 31, and 39).

The story starts 600 years before the birth of the First Emperor and ends 200 years after his death in 210 BC. The exhibition features three sections in chronological order, illustrating the dramatic change from war to peacetime during the first millennium BC. The first section tells the story of how a small and marginal noble family of the First Emperor's ancestors rose to become a powerful state at the dawn of unification. The second section focuses on the First Emperor's afterlife. The artifacts in this section are from the latest archaeological discoveries in the emperor's tomb complex. Magnificent full-sized sculptures include generals, foot soldiers, horses, and an entertainer.

The third section presents the peaceful life of the Han dynasty (206 BC–AD 220). During this period essential Chinese traditions were established that are still reflected in modern Chinese society. The Han emperors continued the First Emperor's administrative policies and also imitated his burial practices. They too buried terracotta soldiers to serve them in the afterlife, although theirs were much smaller in stature. However, the Han rulers had some additional objectives: charming miniature animals, for example,

The existing First Emperor's burial mound

signify a practical wish to maintain herds and flocks in the next world.

THE LIFE of the First Emperor was little known to Western audiences before the discovery of the terracotta warrior pits in 1974. In China, however, he has always been mentioned prominently in historical documents. The earliest account of his life is provided by Sima Qian, who lived about a century after the First Emperor. As court historian of Emperor Wu (156–87 BC), Sima Qian (c. 145–87 BC) completed his *Shiji* (Records of the Grand Historian) in 130 chapters covering 3,000 years of history and legend before his time. The sections devoted to the First Emperor give most of the details we know about his reign.

Today's historians and archaeologists find Sima Qian's written records increasingly trustworthy, since many have now been substantiated by archaeological discoveries. Unearthed oracle bones and bronze vessels with inscriptions dating long before his time verify the historical events and figures he describes, as do the first two objects in the exhibition (see pages 19 and 20). Yet it seems his work was not totally comprehensive. Nowhere, for instance, does he mention the enormous undertaking that produced about 8,000 life-sized terracotta figures.

While the First Emperor's secrecy could be a factor, there might be other reasons for Sima Qian's silence on the matter. Because the

Ongoing archaeological excavation at the terracotta army Pit No. 1

historian served an emperor whose ancestors overthrew the First Emperor's brief dynasty, he had to be conscious of presenting the past in a way that would not distress his ruler with unflattering comparisons. In Han times too,

Confucianism, which became the mainstream ruling doctrine, was strongly at odds with the legalist form of government advocated by the First Emperor. According to Sima Qian, the First Emperor had Confucian scholars executed and burned their books, a story that influenced later historians to treat him as a ruthless tyrant. But even his greatest detractors could not deny his extraordinary achievements and astonishing legacy. Many of these achievements are not only recorded in Sima Qian's writing, but are now known from archaeological discoveries.

SIMA QIAN'S account indicates the earliest Qin settlements were in today's Gansu province, where archaeological finds have now identified their early presence. According to Sima Qian, the Qin moved their political centres or state capitals gradually eastward nine times for strategic military reasons. Following his clues, in the last two or three decades, archaeologists have been able to confirm most

of these historical locations. Some artifacts exhibited come from archaeological sites in capital ruins at Qian (776–762 BC), Pingyang (714–677 BC), Yongcheng (677–383 BC), and Xianyang (350–206 BC). These finds enable us to recognize Qin creativity in some unique art objects (see pages 24 and 25), including the pendants used by a Qin duke (see page 18), and the very rare wall painting from an imperial palace (see page 33).

This archaeological evidence also reveals social changes in the Warring States period (480–221 BC) as the dukes of Qin began their deliberate program of reform. One measure initiated by the Qin dukes was suppression of the practice of human sacrifice associated with major burials, which probably encouraged the creation and widespread use of terracotta human figures as substitutes. The earliest terracotta figures displayed (see pages 28 and 29) include soldiers and attendants, which, though small in size, provide archaeological testimony for this change.

In the 4th century BC, Qin underwent a social revolution engineered by a determined minister, Shang Yang. All of his reforms were intended to maximize order, efficiency, and military strength, and they enabled Qin to grow in power and extent, paving the way for the First Emperor's successful unification. Until recently, Shang Yang was known only from Sima Qian's records and a work on government attributed to him. But in the late 1990s, archaeological evidence, in the form of architectural pieces bearing the character *Shang*, came to light from sites in southeast Shaanxi province, confirming the account that territory there was awarded to Lord Shang by the duke of Xiao in 340 BC. One such object (see page 26) has never been displayed before in any museum.

CONSTRUCTION OF the First Emperor's tomb lasted nearly 40 years, and, according to Sima Qian, involved more than 700,000 labourers. The burial site was well known and was probably partially looted or damaged in the past. Only since the 1970s have modern archaeological techniques been applied to investigating the tomb area. After a few decades of fieldwork, we now know that the terracotta warrior pits formed a very small and peripheral part of a huge site, where more than 500 archaeological components (burials, architectural units like walls and gates, foundation ruins, etc.) have so far been identified. About

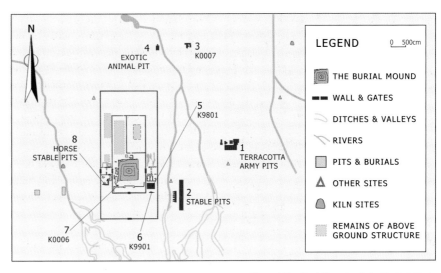

Plan of the First Emperor's tomb complex

Stone armour and helmet excavated *in situ*

180 earth pits—including the terracotta warriors—are distributed inside and outside a double-walled enclosure, a north-south rectangle about 2 square kilometres in area. The great tomb mound itself is central to the compound, located within the inner wall. Accompanying burials have been found in the southern part of the enclosure, while ruins of architecture—remains of funeral temples, residences, administrative offices, and facilities for the tomb construction—are located to the north.

Nearly 2,000 full-sized terracotta warriors and horses have been unearthed from the three pits with a total area of 21,000 square metres, located 1.5 kilometres east of the outer wall. Infantry formations and chariot soldiers are in Pit No.1, while archers and cavalrymen are stationed in Pit No. 2. The small U-shaped Pit No. 3 is a field command post. The exact number of full-sized figures is not certain, as excavations are still ongoing, but about 8,000 figures have been estimated based on the arrangement of military formations. Every so often a few newly restored, full-sized warriors are revealed, explaining why we are able to show some new figures with preserved colours, exclusive to the Canadian exhibition (see page 43).

The accidental discovery of the terracotta army in 1974 was just the beginning of major finds at the site. Since then, more stunning discoveries continually reveal aspects of the

First Emperor's life. Two half-sized, beautifully decorated bronze vehicles were excavated in 1980, unique treasures now permanently installed in the gallery of the Emperor Qin Shihuang's Terracotta Army Museum in Xi'an. Recently, other full-sized terracotta figures were uncovered: from a pit containing civil officials that probably represents the emperor's Department of Justice; from the acrobat pit that represents imperial entertainment; and from the pit with bronze birds and musicians that reproduces the emperor's water garden. A massive armoury with supplies of stone armour was found in a pit larger than the terracotta Pit No.1. Artifacts from these new archaeological sites are also on display (see pages 49–53 and 55).

ARCHAEOLOGY CONFIRMS Sima Qian's observation that the Han emperors continued innovations begun by the First Emperor. Han imperial tombs, though smaller, are clearly modelled on his, with an earthen mound, perimeter wall, shrines and other buildings above ground, and numerous pits underground. A satellite town accompanied each of them, supporting the annual cycle of rituals and sacrifices for the deceased that took place there. Excavations at the tomb complex of the fourth Han emperor Jing (r. 157–141 BC) at Yangling (the satellite town) started in the late 1990s and continue inside the site museum. They have revealed accompanying burials holding a small-sized terracotta army, civil officials, attendants, eunuchs, and clay sculptures of various animals (see artifacts in Section 3). What lies directly beneath the principal Han mounds is unknown, however; like the First Emperor's tomb, they remain unexcavated.

One of the five Chinese Classics, *The Book of Rites*, attributed to Confucius (c. 551–479 BC), counsels: "Serve the dead as you would have served them when living." The First Emperor, however, was a revolutionary in death as well as in life. Rather than simply following the tradition of taking many precious objects with him for use in the next world, scholars believe he aimed at nothing less than the re-creation of his entire world in the hereafter. The size, richness, and complexity of his tomb site far outdid anything constructed either before or after. It appears that Han emperors desired the same thing in the afterlife, but presented it in a more symbolic way.

Han burial customs may offer clues to what archaeologists could find in the First Emperor's tomb mound, should it ever be excavated. The exhibition ends with a painted stone doorway to a burial chamber in a Han grave, a "door to eternity" (see page 67). Perhaps a similar gateway leads into the afterlife residence of Qin Shihuangdi.

THE EXHIBITION

Han Emperor Jing's burial mound

THE RISE OF QIN
(9TH CENTURY–221 BC)

"Qin began as a small state situated in a far-off region, shunned by the Xia lineage [central Chinese] states and classed with the Rong and Di barbarians. But after the time of Duke Xian, it was always a leader among the feudal rulers. . . . In the end it united the whole world under its rule. This was not necessarily due to its mountain barriers or the advantages of its geographic situation. Rather it was as though Heaven had aided it."

— Sima Qian (c. 145–87 BC),
The Records of the Grand Historian, Chapter 15

Translated by Burton Watson: Records of the Grand Historian: Qin Dynasty

This jade pendant was used by Duke Jing of Qin, who lived about 350 years before the birth of the First Emperor. Di 4.9 cm Shaanxi Institute of Archaeology

Ding Tripod

Bronze 1046–771 BC Ht. 45.6 Di. 39.4 Dp. 20 cm
Baoji Bronze Museum

In Bronze Age China (c. 20th–3rd century BC), bronze *ding* tripods were among ceremonial vessels used by noble families to offer food to gods or ancestors. Inscriptions on such vessels frequently commemorated the family's illustrious history, and they were passed from generation to generation. The owner of this vessel, Shan Lai, was given responsibility for governing a territory by King Xuan (r. 827–782 BC), and had a set of ten *ding* vessels in graduated sizes, with inscriptions of 316 characters on each, cast to record the event.

According to Sima Qian, the First Emperor's ancestor, Qin Zhong, also served the same King Xuan, but as an official in charge of horse breeding for the Zhou Kingdom. He held lower rank and had weaker association with the king. His noble family, the Ying, was not enfeoffed or given any state title until several decades later.

Bell of the Duke of Qin

Bronze   771–481 BC   Ht. 69.6 Wi. 28.4 cm
Baoji Bronze Museum

"My foremost ancestor received the Mandate of Heaven, was awarded land and received title to a state . . ."

This 135-character essay was inscribed on a set of three bronze *bo* bells that belonged to Duke Wu of Qin (c. 697–678 BC). The bells were excavated in 1978 from Pingyang, Qin's old capital near today's Baoji, along with another set of five *niu* bells also belonging to the Duke.

Musical bells, normally played in sets, were important ritual objects used in ancient China for ceremonial occasions. This bell, with its elegant openwork flanges, provides the first archaeological evidence verifying historical records that the First Emperor's ancestor, Duke Xiang (c. 780–769 BC), was given official state lordship by the Zhou king. This was done to reward the Ying clan for its military support during the removal of the royal family to the eastern capital Luoyang at the time of the invasion of the Xi Rong people in 771 BC.

He Wine Vessel

Bronze   771–481 BC   Ht. 20 Wi. 21 Dp. 4.5 cm
Longxian County Museum

This wine vessel was recovered from Bianjiazhuang, Longxian County, near the northwestern border of today's Shaanxi province, where the Qin state capital Qian was located during the earlier 8th century BC. When the Qin dukes moved their royal residence to the east in 762 BC, some noble families still remained in this western location. Bianjiazhuang was the family cemetery of the nobility, as indicated by the presence of ritual bronze vessels in burials there, some of them clearly later than the removal of the capital.

The vessel is decorated with prominent bird motifs. A bird with a crest and hooked beak functions as a lid, and a large bird in low relief dominates each flat side. Some scholars consider the bird motif on early bronze vessels of Qin, similar to pottery bird models shown in the exhibition, evidence that the Qin people originated in the East where a bird totem was recognized.

Bridle Fitting

Gold   481–221 BC   Le. 4.1 Wi. 3.4 cm
Fengxiang County Museum

Horses were highly regarded by the Qin people, perhaps reflecting the fact that the First Emperor's ancestors rose to power by breeding horses for the Zhou dynasty rulers in the 9th–8th centuries BC. Horses used by high-status members of the nobility could have been decorated with ornaments like this gold object, which was most likely attached to the bridle of a horse. The openwork fitting is masterfully cast with five intertwined dragons in high relief. On the back is a broad, flattened loop for fitting onto a bridle strap.

Gold from ancient China is rarely found, but a number of small gold ornaments, mostly horse fittings, have been discovered in archaeological sites affiliated with Qin culture. Its appearance there was probably because of the relationship Qin had with nomadic horse breeders on the northwestern frontier, who associated the use of gold with status.

Pendant Set

Jade   771–481 BC   Ht. 7.1 cm
Longxian County Museum

Worn as a necklace, this jade pendant set was found on the body of a Qin nobleman from a 7th century BC burial at Bianjia-zhuang. The set consists of two fish-shaped pendants (*huang* and *pei*), one pointed pendant (*xi*), and a series of agate beads. During the Western Zhou period (c. 1046–771 BC), pendant sets like this were considered by the nobility as appropriate emblems of their rank and were not mere costume accessories. This Qin pendant necklace is still rather simple, as such sets found in feudal states in central China at the time might contain dozens or even hundreds of pendants. It illustrates an aristocratic taste for luxury in the early Qin state, even while it remained less powerful than other states to the east.

Painted Pottery Vessels

Earthenware   221–206 BC   Ht. 24.4 Di. (mouth) 10.4 cm (top)
Ht. 14.2 Di. (base) 15 cm (bottom)
Longxian County Museum

The earliest painted pottery appeared on the east coast of China about 8,000 years ago, and the type became common in the Yellow River Valley around 6,000 to 5,000 years ago. These Qin vessels were painted after being fired, as were the First Emperor's terracotta soldiers and subsequent Han dynasty tomb figures in this exhibit.

The pottery wares shown here are decorated with white and red pigments, in linear designs like spirals, circles, triangles, and feathered patterns on a reddish yellow ground. They represent food containers or wine vessels, but were not made for daily use. Painted pottery was probably utilized during ceremonies or burial rituals by middle-class members of the early Qin State (7th–6th century BC), who were not allowed to use bronze ritual vessels for such occasions.

Wine Vessel with Garlic Mouth

Bronze   206 BC–AD 220   Ht. 26.7 Di. (base) 11.3 cm
Longxian County Museum

This bronze wine vessel, with its swelling body and elongated neck with garlic-shaped mouth, is unique to the Qin tradition. Similarly shaped pottery wine vessels are also found in Qin middle-class burials, presumably used as ritual vessels in that context as well. There are some variations, but all are characterized by the garlic mouth. Such objects are a good indicator of cultural interactions. When garlic-mouth wine vessels are found from burials in Sichuan and Hubei provinces a few hundred kilometres away from the Qin centre, archaeologists can infer that the owners of such burials were Qin migrants.

Roof Tile with Character *Shang*

Earthenware   481–221 BC   Dp. 0.8 Di. 15.5 cm
Shangluo Municipal Museum

Only the closed end of this tile survives; it originally faced outward. It displays the moulded character *Shang* indicating it was used on roofs of residences, temples, or official structures that belonged to Lord Shang (d. 338 BC), a reformer and most influential figure in the Qin state. Recovered in a mountainous region about 300 kilometres south of the Qin capital Xianyang, it is the first archaeological evidence verifying the historical record that Gongsun Yang was given the noble title *jun* (lord) and a territory with 15 cities as his fief by Duke Xiao in 340 BC. In that year, Yang, as chief minister leading a Qin army, won a decisive battle defeating Qin's long-time rival state of Wei, and recovered lands west of the Yellow River previously lost to Wei. Because of this title Lord Shang, Yang is best known in Chinese history as Shang Yang.

Granary Model

Earthenware   221–206 BC   Ht. 23 Di. (base) 12.5 cm
Longxian County Museum

Pottery models of granaries first appeared in Qin middle-class burials during the 6th–5th century BC. By the Han dynasty (206 BC–AD 220), they were commonly found in most tombs of the wealthy. While this round example shows the earliest form, in the Han dynasty rectangular granary models prevailed. The increasing use of such models as burial goods reflects significant social and economic changes in the Qin state, among them a series of land reforms initiated by Shang Yang, a close advisor to Duke Xiao (r. 361–338 BC). As a result, the emerging middle class benefitted from wealth based on private land ownership. Its members ignored Zhou rituals, in which the middle-to-upper class used conventional bronze vessels or bells (see pages 19–21 and 30) or ceramic substitutes, and instead introduced the granary model to symbolize their new prosperity in the rising Qin state.

Cavalry Figures

Earthenware   481–221 BC   Ht. 22.3 cm Le. 18.4 Wi. 18 cm (top)
Ht. 22.6 cm Le.18.4 cm (bottom)
Xianyang Institute of Archaeology and Cultural Relics

These two miniature soldiers riding horses, unearthed from a military official's burial near the Qin city Xianyang, are the earliest terracotta warriors found in China to date. They were made about 100 years before the First Emperor's life-sized figures, and show that cavalry was employed in the Qin state's army during the wars leading to unification. Some of the bronze vessels from the same burial, including the one on display, were made in other states, suggesting that this military official had collected trophies after winning battles.

Both horses and human figures are painted in red over a grey clay surface, with details in black. The eyes and mouth of each soldier are indicated with incised lines, but the nose is modelled in high relief. Each has a hat with a wide, flat sunshade and wears the same uniform: a short robe without armour, short trousers, and boots.

Group of Figures

Earthenware   481–221 BC   Ht. 15 Le. 20.5 cm (horse)
Ht. 7.7–12.5 cm (figures)
Xi'an Institute of Archaeology and Heritage Preservation

This small group includes three standing attendants, one kneeling servant, one dismounted rider, and one horse. All were painted in red and black, with modelled headdress details. The standing horse appears strong and sturdy, and its full tail has a knot at the end. Red lines on its black-painted body represent the saddle and reins.

The group was recently excavated from a Warring States period burial in today's Xi'an, and has not previously been displayed in any museum exhibit. Sets of burial figures indicate that the tomb owner must have been from a wealthy family, though not one with inherited noble status. This clearly illustrates what we know from historical sources—that social changes allowed Qin commoners, or even slaves, to gain wealth by providing military services to the state prior to Qin's unification.

Pictorial *Hu* Wine Vessel

Bronze   481–221 BC   Ht. 40 Di. 12.3 cm
Fengxiang County Museum

A cache of 12 bronze vessels (four in the exhibit) was recovered in 1977 near the royal palace ruins in Yongcheng, a Qin capital city during the 7th–5th centuries BC. Archaeologists believe they represent a royal collection once held in a nearby palace.

This pictorial *hu* is one of a pair in the group. Copper-inlaid scenes from life are arranged in four registers separated by three narrow, decorated, raised bands. The top register illustrates archery contests, shown upside down as if meant to be seen from above. The two middle registers have scenes of archers hunting birds (above) and performing musicians (below). The bottom register depicts a group of hunters.

So far, fewer than a dozen such pictorial *hu* vessels, including one in the Royal Ontario Museum (see page 68), are known. Although they were recovered from different sites, they were all manufactured in central China in a territory of the state of Jin.

Wine Vessel

Lacquered earthenware   771–481 BC   Ht. 33 Di. 13.3 cm
Shangluo Municipal Museum

Lacquer vessels and utensils became common in southern China during the Warring States period. This wine container has a thin pottery body, with designs in red and white painted on a black lacquer ground. Similar to some bronze vessels of the period, this lacquered *hu* has a lid with a corona of six flaring lotus leaves rising from it. The body is decorated with eight panels filled with angular and spiral designs.

The Qin state embraced changes in the arts as much as in the economy and government. This lacquer was unearthed in southeast Shaanxi, from land once belonging to Lord Shang Yang. Yang encouraged immigration, with the aim of increasing the agricultural prosperity and military strength of Qin. Characteristic of craftsmanship in the neighbouring Chu state to the south, the use of lacquer exemplified Qin's openness toward foreigners and new ideas through either immigration or adoption.

Palace Wall Painting

Clay   221–206 BC   Le. 78 Wi. 46 cm
Shaanxi Institute of Archaeology

Remember the fabled palaces of Xianyang
Shimmering with beauty from six fallen states,
The emperor, intoxicated with such loveliness,
Forgetting to mind affairs in far mountains and river ways.

Xianyang, poem by Li Shangying, Tang dynasty (AD 618–906)

Legends say that the First Emperor built more than 300 palaces in Xianyang, the Qin's last capital for 144 years. Many replicated royal architecture from all the states his armies had conquered. For decades, archaeologists have been investigating the ruins of Xianyang, and so far, four palaces have been excavated. The reconstruction of Palace No. 1, the model displayed in the exhibit, shows compounds of three-storey buildings, connected and surrounded by covered corridors. The walls of such roofed corridors in Palaces 1, 2, and 3 were painted with animals, flowers and plants, human figures, geometric patterns, and scenes from life. Second only to the discovery of the terracotta warriors, these wall paintings are among the greatest finds from the First Emperor's lifetime.

Hundreds of mural fragments were recovered among the remains of collapsed walls, broken into such small pieces that their subjects are hard to identify. This example is among the few that are large and relatively well preserved. A diamond-shaped panel is contained within a black frame that opens and turns inward at one corner to form a traditional Chinese cloud pattern. Within the frame, a pair of tan-coloured horses is drawing a two-wheeled carriage and driver. While earlier evidence of this theme is lacking, running horse-drawn carriages were to become common in later wall paintings and relief sculptures found in Han dynasty tombs.

This colourful wall painting is the earliest example of its kind found so far in China.

Roof Tile with Decorated End, and Decorated Ends

Earthenware 771–481 BC Di. 16.5 cm (top left) Di. 15.5 cm (top right) Le. 40 Di. 10.5 cm (bottom)
Shaanxi Institute of Archaeology (top row), Fengxiang County Museum

Grander Qin structures, such as temples, palaces, and official buildings, usually had roof tiles with decorated ends where they terminated at the eaves. The designs on these are unique to the Qin and continued to be used in the following Han dynasty. Animals were favourite subjects for this decoration; the example on the top right depicts a tiger hunting a deer, while the one on the top left shows five animals (deer, fawn, dog, toad, and wild goose).

Chinese mythic animals like the dragon and the auspicious phoenix were also common in roof tile decoration, as seen in the lower illustration. According to the *Er Ya*, the earliest Chinese encyclopedia of animals and plants, probably compiled during the 3rd–2nd century BC, a phoenix was said to have a "rooster's head, swallow's face, snake's neck, turtle's back, and fish's tail."

Incense Burner

Earthenware 481–221 BC Ht. 17 Le. 21 cm
Shaanxi Institute of Archaeology

Found in a Qin burial in the city of Xianyang, the function of this unique grey earthenware vessel is still debated. Scholars now believe it could be an incense burner.

It represents a horse carrying a cylindrical burner chamber. The horse's legs were broken and the ends then flattened. The burner is hollow with a grate at the bottom. A large toad and a small dog are on the lid, the toad serving as a handle for the rear part, which opens. The burner chamber is decorated with crossed lines outside and fish designs inside. The bodies of the two facing animals on the lid are hollow (as is that of the horse) and communicate with the interior. The animals' mouths, in addition to 12 holes on the back of the toad, would allow incense smoke to escape.

Trigger Mechanism and Model of Crossbow

Bronze   221–206 BC   Le. 16 Wi. 2.1 cm (top)
Wood   Le. 143 Wi. 86 cm (bottom)
Emperor Qin Shihuang's Terracotta Army Museum

Crossbows, which have a bow mounted on a stock along which the string is drawn, are among the most lethal weapons of antiquity. Their accuracy and penetrating power gave armies using them a considerable advantage. However, archers had to pause and draw the string with both arms, either standing or sitting with feet braced against the bow.

Early Chinese crossbows, probably adopted from southern China or Southeast Asia, seem to have been lighter and used mainly in hunting. They appear in Chinese burials of the Warring States period, and became common in the 4th–3rd centuries BC after the metal trigger mechanism was adopted. By the Qin dynasty, crossbow archers formed part of the imperial army's battle formation. The crossbow units among the terracotta soldiers were originally equipped with functional examples similar to this modern reproduction.

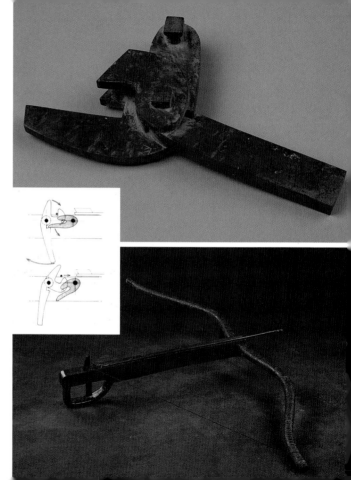

Inlaid Belt Hook

Gilt Bronze, Shell   481–221 BC   Ht. 5 Le. 23.4 Wi. 3.4 cm
Xi'an Municipal Museum

Bronze and jade belt hooks were used by men in later Bronze Age China, both for function and as stylish personal accessories. Often plain, they could also be richly ornamental, or even made into representations of animals, such as the monkey shown in the exhibition. Images of various belt hooks can be seen on the terracotta warrior figures.

At both ends of this rare gilt bronze example, animal heads are depicted in detail, with large eyes, prominent snouts, and broad mouths. Notably, both pairs of eyes are inlaid with black glass beads. The animals' bodies stretch back toward the middle of the object, holding three shell inlays.

Though buried in Qin territory where its owner apparently served as an official, characters inscribed on this belt hook, as well as the presence in his tomb of typical bronze and lacquer objects, indicate that he came from the Chu state in the south.

Plaque and Moulds

Bronze   481–221 BC   Le. 10.8 Wi. 5.5 cm (top left)
Shaanxi History Museum

Earthenware   221–206 BC   Le. 5.2 Wi. 4.2 Dp. 0.6 cm (middle left)
Le. 7.9 Wi. 6.7 Dp. 1.4 cm (middle right) Le. 7 cm (bottom left) Le. 9.4
Wi. 7 Dp. 2.5 cm (bottom right)
Shaanxi Institute of Archaeology

Because of its location in the west, the Qin state had extensive contact with ethnic groups in the farther northwest (*Xi Rong*) and southwest (*Ba* and *Dian*), and absorbed much of their distinctive art. The gilt bronze plaque with a bull in relief (top left) was produced by the Dian people, near today's Kunming, Yunnan province. Similar ornaments were also common among the northwestern nomads, where images of camels, deer, and dragons were most often seen. While these products were readily accepted through trade and exchange, local versions were also produced by Qin craftsmen in their own styles.

For the first time, a set of clay moulds for casting such bronze plaques has been recovered from a Qin dynasty burial near Xi'an. The site included moulds for a variety of objects, such as horse and chariot fittings, lamps, knives, and crossbow fittings. The discovery of a burial in which more than half the objects found were clay moulds suggests that it belonged to a craftsman who supplied moulds for bronze manufacturing. Bronze plaques cast from these moulds would bear motifs unique to their locality.

A mould with human figures depicts a woman wearing non-traditional Chinese robes and headdress, holding a boy with a ball at his feet (bottom left). Two sheep with large curved horns and extended rear legs are arranged symmetrically on another mould (middle right). A horse is vividly depicted with hindquarters twisted upwards, its hoof touching its mane (bottom right). The oval plaque (middle left) shows a scene of a flying eagle attacked by two tigers. Two mythic animals, with bird heads and snake bodies, are shown above the tigers' heads.

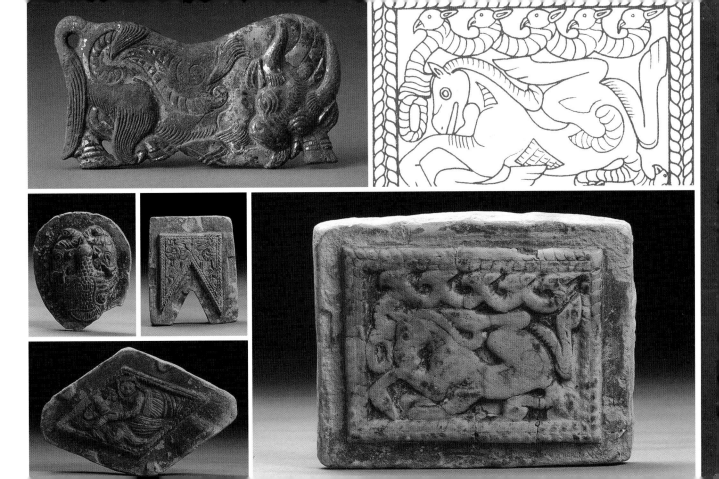

THE TERRACOTTA ARMY
(221–206 BC)

"Insignificant as I am, I have raised troops to punish the rebellious princes; and thanks to the sacred power of our ancestors, all six kings have been chastised as they deserved, so that at last the empire is pacified. Now if some change in title is not carried out, there will be no way to celebrate these achievements and make them known to later generations. Let deliberations be held on an imperial title."

— The First Emperor, quoted by Sima Qian (c.145–87 BC),
The Records of the Grand Historian, Chapter 6
Translated by Burton Watson: Records of the Grand Historian: Qin Dynasty

Infantry Soldier

Earthenware 221–206 BC Ht. 189 cm
Emperor Qin Shihuang's Terracotta Army Museum

Of an estimated 8,000 figures originally buried in the three terracotta warrior pits, over 1,000 low-ranking soldiers, with and without armour, have been unearthed. Their postures, either standing
or kneeling, and their costumes are more or less the same, but the
fact that each of them expresses such individuality and personality
is impressive. The level of detail has suggested to some observers
that each of the terracotta warriors could have been modelled from
a living soldier. Every figure, whether young or old, shows vividly
his pride, loyalty, seriousness, concern, yearning, or even sadness.

This soldier from the light infantry has no armour, but he
probably held a bow. Like most other foot soldiers, he wears short
trousers and puttees (leather or cloth strips wound around the
lower legs).

Armoured General

Earthenware 221–206 BC Ht. 196 cm
Emperor Qin Shihuang's Terracotta Army Museum

Only nine figures of generals, the highest ranking commanders in the Qin Emperor's army, have been recovered so far. Each has a distinctive appearance, with flaring twin-peaked headgear, intricate armour of fish-scale design, a double-layered tunic, and flat-ended shoes with upturned toes; these features distinguish the figure of the general from the more than 1,000 soldiers unearthed from the three pits. His height, and the prominent knotted bows, tied in pairs to the front, shoulders, and back of the armour, also clearly denote the highest military rank.

When unearthed, this general stood on a command chariot. Watching his troops from above, his eyes are half-closed, reserved, and confident. His right hand crosses over to hold the other wrist while the palm of the left hand once rested on the handle of a long sword pointing to the ground in front of him. The general's imperious expression suggests authority and determination, as if he is ready to command a battle for his emperor.

Kneeling Archer

Earthenware 221–206 BC Ht. 130 cm
Emperor Qin Shihuang's Terracotta Army Museum

The Qin army had a large contingent of archers who employed powerful and deadly crossbows (see page 36). This half-kneeling archer is one of 332 found in Pit No. 2, lined up in battle formation. In combat, archers were arrayed in rows, one row firing arrows from a standing position while the others knelt to arm their crossbows. This kneeling soldier has both hands at the right side of his body to hold a crossbow. He looks down as if he is taking a breath, ready to stand up for the next round of shooting.

Most of the earthenware figures from early excavations are grey in appearance, but they were originally painted with bright colours—green, red, purple, blue, and white. Conservation techniques used in excavating Pit No. 2 in the 1990s preserved this rare example of a figure with some intact colours.

Unarmoured general. Ht. 199 cm Emperor Qin Shihuang's Terracotta Army Museum

Charioteer and Horse

Earthenware 221–206 BC   Ht. 190 cm (charioteer)
Ht. 166 Le. 193 cm (horse)
Emperor Qin Shihuang's Terracotta Army Museum

Chariots were already common on the battlefields of China before the time of the First Emperor. By the Qin unification, chariots had apparently become an elite division of the First Emperor's army. All charioteers from the terracotta warrior pits held official rank, as indicated by their flat headdress, and drove chariots pulled by four horses. The charioteer, then called *yushou* (royal driver), controlled and directed the formations of foot soldiers.

Each chariot also carried one or two soldiers who would have fought with a medium-range weapon like a *ge* dagger-axe over the moving wheels. Because the charioteer would not be able to defend himself while holding the reins, most wore special armour, with sleeves that extended over the hands and a high collar to protect the neck. However, our charioteer in the exhibition bravely wears just the armour of a regular soldier.

A few charioteers had the honour of driving a command chariot containing a general (see page 42) and a guard. Such a chariot would also have contained a leather drum and a bronze bell (see example in the exhibition) used by the general for directing military movements. Slight differences between cavalry and chariot horses found with the terracotta army suggest that in life they were specially selected for their roles.

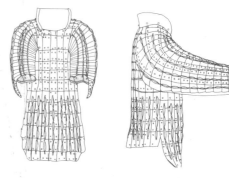

Cavalry Horse and Soldier

Earthenware   221–206 BC   Ht. 172 Le. 203 cm (horse)
Ht. 184 cm (soldier)
Emperor Qin Shihuang's Terracotta Army Museum

Two kinds of horses, both for the battlefield, were found in the terracotta pits: horses for mounted cavalry, and horses for pulling the war chariots. This cavalry horse is beautifully outfitted, with its saddle showing ornamental studs, girth strap, and crupper. It was ridden without stirrups, which did not come into use until later centuries. The head is modelled in extremely fine detail—with flared nostrils, skin creases around the wide-open eyes, ears pitched forward and alert, and mouth slightly open—presenting great character and realism. Its remarkable size matches that of the real horses buried near the First Emperor's tomb.

In battle, a unit of the First Emperor's cavalry was likely deployed to the rear of the military formation, as displayed in Pit No. 2, where 116 saddle horses were found in this position, each accompanied by a standing cavalry soldier.

Civil Official

Earthenware   221–206 BC   Ht. 188 cm
Shaanxi Institute of Archaeology

In 2000, archaeologists discovered a new pit with life-sized terra-cotta figures at the southwestern corner of the First Emperor's tomb complex, very close to the mound itself. This time, it held not soldiers but civil officials. Their high rank is suggested by both the distinctive cap and the flat-ended shoes with raised toes, exactly like those of the armoured figure of a general in the exhibition. Their hands are tucked into the long sleeves of their robes. Each official has a knife and sharpening stone hanging from the right side of his waist, necessary tools for working on the bamboo strips or wooden tablets used for writing at the time. A wooden tablet was likely slipped into the space between the left arm and chest, just as we would now carry a file folder or notepad to a meeting. Archaeologists believe this pit represented an administrative office, probably the Department of Justice.

Armour and Helmet

Stone   221–206 BC   Ht. 77 Wi. 50 cm (armour)
Ht. 38 Wi. 21 cm (helmet)
Shaanxi Institute of Archaeology

Stone armour and helmets were not used for actual combat. A suit is extremely heavy, weighing as much as 20 kilograms, as it could have more than 600 limestone plaques linked together with copper wires. Yet hundreds of life-sized suits were made and buried specially for the First Emperor's underworld army. Real armour and helmets used in the Warring States period were made from iron or leather.

Found in 1999 at the southeast corner of the tomb complex, Pit K9801 is as large as the terracotta warrior Pit No. 1, but only one-eightieth of it has been excavated, revealing 87 suits and 43 helmets. It is hard to imagine how many more suits there could be, and in what variety, if the pit were excavated entirely. It appears that the huge quantity of armour buried would have been sufficient to outfit the 8,000 terracotta warriors. However, none of the terracotta warriors wear helmets, possibly to demonstrate their bravery in the service of the First Emperor.

Reconstruction of these suits is extremely time-consuming, since all were found collapsed. The wooden stands or hanging frames on which they were probably mounted originally had disintegrated long ago.

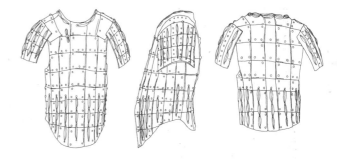

Acrobat

Earthenware   221–206 BC   Ht. 180 Wi. (shoulder) 30 cm (right)
Emperor Qin Shihuang's Terracotta Army Museum

Earthenware   1st–2nd century AD   Ht. 21.2 Wi. 10.2 cm (juggler, left, ROM artifact)
George Crofts Collection

Acrobats were familiar entertainers in the royal court during the Han dynasty (206 BC–AD 220), as recorded in early historic documents and indicated by many tomb figures of acrobats (see the ROM example at left). Such performances in China may have originated in the Warring States period, or even earlier. Ancient documents referred to acrobats as *bai xi*, literally "hundred games," and Emperor Wu (156–87 BC) encouraged acrobatic games as sporting competitions. Archaeological finds illustrate well over a dozen different types of performance. This tradition has lasted to the present day; China is widely recognized as having the most sophisticated acrobatic performers in the world.

This life-sized acrobat, also called a "*bai xi* terracotta," is our earliest archaeological evidence that such entertainment existed in the Qin dynasty. It was recently recovered from an accompanying pit, K9901, at the southeast corner of the First Emperor's tomb complex. The total area of the pit is about 800 square metres, and the first excavation in 1999 unearthed 11 acrobat figures, all full-sized, from a test pit only 9 square metres large. Though all are incomplete, their postures show various kinds of performance for the emperor. The figure in the exhibition is the only one of the 11 retaining part of his head. His face shows an expression of calm concentration on his performance, which probably involved balancing weight by using one finger of his right hand. In his right index finger, there is a hole 0.4 centimetres in diameter running down to the palm, indicating that something like a rod was inserted. Missing the left arm and the left leg, the figure wears nothing but a simple skirt, the same costume as his companions found in the pit. His right leg is bent backward with the toe touching the ground, a suitable stance for a balancing act.

Swan

Bronze 221–206 BC Ht. 100 Le. 90 Wi. 50 cm
Shaanxi Institute of Archaeology

The most recent discovery of full-sized figures from the First Emperor's tomb complex is Pit K0007, an F-shaped underground chamber with three sections. The floor of the longest section was paved with wooden planks covered with clay plaster, and the excavators believe it represented a river; on its wooden banks were found 46 life-sized bronze waterfowl, including six cranes, 20 swans, and 20 wild geese. Most birds' heads face the "river," except for a few found in its middle. They are in different positions: standing, resting, looking for food, and one even eating a worm.

In another section, 15 full-sized terracotta figures were found. These figures, dressed as servants, seem to be playing musical instruments, now missing. The excavation in 2001 revealed that the pit had been burned, so that only bronze and pottery figures survived. Some scholars believe the group represents an underground pleasure garden for the First Emperor.

THE HARMONIOUS HAN
(206 BC–AD 220)

"In the reign of Emperor Hui [221–188 BC, r. 194–188 BC] . . . the common people succeeded in putting behind them the sufferings of the age of the Warring States and ruler and subject alike sought rest in surcease of action. Therefore . . . the world was at peace. Punishments were seldom meted out and evildoers grew rare, while the people applied themselves to the tasks of farming, and food and clothing became abundant."

— Sima Qian (c.145–87 BC),
The Records of the Grand Historian, Chapter 9
Translated by Burton Watson: Records of the Grand Historian: Han Dynasty

This kneeling female figure in painted terracotta was recovered from a burial within the tomb complex of Emperor Jing at Yangling. Emperor Jing (r. 157–141 BC) was the grandson of Emperor Hui. Ht. 41 Wi. (shoulder) 11.5 cm Hanyangling Museum

Han Emperor's Cavalry and Infantry

Earthenware   206 BC–AD 220   Ht. 58 Le. 50 Wi. 17 cm (top)
Ht. 50 Wi. 15 Dp. 11 cm (bottom)
Xianyang Museum

In 1965, archaeologists excavated a terracotta warrior pit at Yangjia-wan near the tomb complex of Emperor Gaozu, who established the Han dynasty in 206 BC. The pit contained 1,800 infantry-man and 580 cavalrymen. Foot soldiers about 50 centimetres tall wear painted red caps tied under the chin and black chest armour over short white robes. Most held a long-shafted wooden weapon, now vanished, in one hand and a shield in the other. The cavalry figures are in two different sizes, possibly representing two differ-ent functions for cavalry described in texts of the period—frontal attacks and penetration of the opposing army's flanks.

    The discovery of Emperor Gaozu's terracotta army at Yangjiawan revealed that large changes had taken place in mil-itary organization. Where the First Emperor had a sizable chariot component, the early Han army mainly utilized infantry in mass formation, supplemented with several cavalry units.

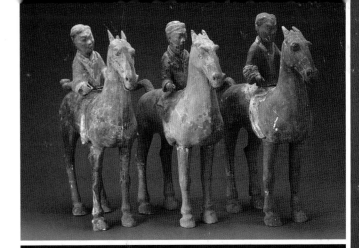

Cavalry Figures

Earthenware 206 BC–AD 220 Ht. 58.3 Wi. 9.3 cm (left)
Ht. 56 cm (right) Ht. 8 cm (top)
Hanyangling Museum

Unlike earlier examples from the time of the First Emperor and Emperor Gaozu of the Han dynasty, many thousands of cavalry figures found within the tomb complex of Emperor Jing (r. 156–140 BC) at Yangling originally had wooden arms and horses. The painting on the terracotta figures was relatively well preserved, retaining orange colour on the faces, bodies, and legs, while black lines were drawn on the hair, eyebrows, and eyes. All Yangling examples wore military clothing, which was not preserved; the hair of the warrior head (above centre) has clear textile impressions, indicating a red textile headdress.

Ancient texts confirm that women served in the military, even in Han dynasty cavalry units. The sex of these figures is determined mainly by their distinctive hairstyles; females have a bun at the back (right), while males have a central part and short hair.

Eunuch

Earthenware   206 BC–AD 220   Ht. 57 Wi. (shoulder) 9.31 cm
Hanyangling Museum

Like many of Emperor Jing's soldiers, this terracotta figure when buried had arms (probably of wood) and wore textile clothing, both of which had disintegrated. This figure is not a soldier, however, but one of the Emperor's eunuchs, identified by his modified genitals. Employment of eunuchs at court to serve the rulers and especially their female companions was a continuous practice, probably beginning during the Western Zhou period (1046–771 BC) and lasting to the end of the Qing dynasty (AD 1911). In many historical periods, including the later Han dynasty, eunuchs used their proximity to the emperors to undermine the power of the administrative officials, thereby inevitably changing the course of Chinese history.

This is the earliest archaeological evidence found so far demonstrating the existence of eunuchs in the early Han dynasty.

Male Figure

Earthenware   206 BC–AD 220   Ht. 63 Wi. (base) 23 cm
Hanyangling Museum

Found in an accompanying burial of Emperor Jing at the Yangling tomb complex, this male figure was fully painted in soft colours. Red is obvious along the borders of the double-layered white robe he is wearing and seems to represent an embroidered or patterned band. He wears a black headdress and a pair of boat-shaped shoes. Under his left arm there is a thin slit for inserting a wood or bamboo tablet, used for record keeping. With neat eyebrows and moustache, the gentleman looks composed and deferential, making him appear to be an assistant or advisory official to the emperor or high-ranking administrators. With his hands clasped inside his sleeves, he stands ready to report for assignment.

Female Figure

Earthenware   206 BC–AD 220   Ht. 63 Wi. (base) 25 cm
Hanyangling Museum

This female figure was unearthed from the same burial at Yangling as the male figure (see page 60) and probably represents an attendant to a noble lady. She is neatly dressed in fine multi-layered robes, the outer ones with red borders similar to those on the garment worn by the male. These borders and the red waistband contrast with her white robe with its flaring hem. Her hands hidden by full sleeves, she stands with relaxed knees and head tilted modestly forward. She has a round, pretty face and pleasant expression, and long hair falls down her back, gathered into a knot at the end.

Some actual Han dynasty garments have survived in a woman's burial near Changsha in former Chu state territory. They confirm the style seen here of a wrap-over robe worn on top of layered undergarments, and indicate the rich textures and colouring of dress at the time.

Goose

Earthenware   206 BC–AD 220   Ht. 22 Le. 38.5 Wi. 12 cm
Xi'an Municipal Museum

Painted ceramic animal figures are very common in the Han dynasty, mostly found as funerary goods in well-furnished Han tombs. This small sculpture demonstrates the high level of artistic craftsmanship available at the time for making even ordinary objects. Incised lines with red paint vividly depict the characteristics of this resting goose. A simple painted circle and two curved lines delineate the bird's head with its flat beak. On the body, a painted spiral leads into rows of scale-like patterns outlined in red, representing its feathers. Its wings reach toward its tail, which is extended to steady the base. A hole in the top of its head suggests that the sculpture could once have supported something, perhaps a lamp. Its overall appearance indicates the bird may represent a wild swan goose (*Anser cygnoides*), native to this part of the world.

Seals and Seal Impression

Clay (top left), Bronze (top right)   206 BC–AD 220   Ht. 0.57 Le. 0.91
Wi. 0.87 cm (right) Le. 3.8 Wi. 1.93 Dp. 1.38 cm (left)
Hanyangling Museum

The script on the seals and on the clay seal impression represents the writing style *lishu* (clerk's script), standardized after the First Emperor's unification. Before the invention of paper in the early 2nd century AD, official correspondence was written on bamboo strips or silk, and sealed with finely processed clay.

The bronze seal on the right belonged to an official responsible for duties in the Changle Palace, a place well known in historical texts. The four recessed characters produced a raised impression on sealing clay, like the example shown on the left. The clay is well preserved, clearly showing the four characters *Yangling Lingyin* (seal of Yangling Civic Official), referring to the official in charge of administrative affairs in the satellite town near Emperor Jing's tomb complex. On the back of the clay is an impression of bamboo strips, suggesting that the object was used for sealing an official document written on a roll of bamboo strips.

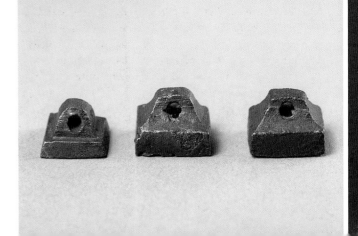

Dogs

Earthenware   206 BC–AD 220   Ht. 19.9 Le. 31.2 Wi. 8.5 cm (top)
Ht. 19.9 Le. 35 Wi. 9.2 cm (bottom)
Hanyangling Museum

Five dogs have been included in the exhibition out of 456 painted examples recovered from Pit No. 13, one of many accompanying burials within Emperor Jing's tomb complex at Yangling. Two types of dog are represented here, the first with a heavy head and neck, longer legs and a hanging tail, and the second, a female, with its tail curled up on its back.

Dogs are among the earliest domesticated animals in China, where archaeological evidence for their domestication in central China can be traced back 9,000 years. Besides being trained for guarding and hunting, they were often living sacrifices used in rituals and ancestor worship. In the First Emperor's tomb complex, no designated pits of terracotta dogs or other farmyard animals have yet been found. Only horses and wild birds seem to have been chosen for burial there.

Rooster and Hen

Earthenware   206 BC–AD 220   Ht. 15 Le. 15.5 cm (rooster)
Ht. 12 Le. 15 cm (hen)
Shaanxi Institute of Archaeology

Pit No. 13 at Yangling contained not only many dogs, but also
other domestic animals like sheep, goats, and pigs, some of them
also shown in the exhibition. Roosters and hens were also present but found in extremely low numbers. However, for some rea-
son, their painted colours of red and yellow are better preserved
than those of other animals. Since all the chickens were originally
modelled on wooden legs that had decayed, the legs seen here are
modern replacements.

Brazier

Earthenware   206 BC–AD 220   Ht. 8.3 Le. 24.6 Wi 17.6 cm
Shaanxi History Museum

People at the time called objects like this brazier *mingqi*, literally "utensils for the afterlife." In the Han dynasty, models of practical things used during life were commonly made for burial in the multiple-chambered brick tombs, reflecting the desire for a peaceful and prosperous lifestyle to continue. Many images depicted on tomb bricks also show that roasting over a fire was a popular cooking method in ancient China, especially in the Han dynasty.

This brazier has four supports in the shape of bears. The surface is modelled in relief with rings representing handles, and running animals. The bottom of the firebox is perforated for removal of ashes, indicating use of a charcoal or wood fire. Most intriguing is the representation of two skewers, with four cicadas on each. Apparently, grilled cicada must already have been considered a delicacy in Han times.

Tomb Gate

Stone   206 BC–AD 220   Le. 193.5 Wi. 35.5 Dp. 6 cm (top frame)
Le. 122.5 Wi. 31 Dp. 6 cm (left column) Le. 121 Wi. 32.5 Dp. 6 cm
(right column) Le. 113 Wi. 48.5 Dp. 4.5 cm (left door) Le. 113.5 Wi.
48.5 Dp. 4 cm (right door)
Shaanxi Institute of Archaeology

Han dynasty tombs of the wealthy were regularly constructed using pictorial stones or bricks. At Shengmu Dabaodang in northern Shaanxi province, archaeologists discovered a Han family cemetery where many of the tombs had stones with painted pictorial reliefs. The tomb gate in the exhibit consists of five stone panels, comprising a horizontal lintel, two vertical side pieces, and two doors.

Many scenes depicted represent the "three worlds" of individual experience according to Chinese belief at the time: a heavenly realm, an actual lifetime, and an underground afterlife. On the top, hunting scenes and a family procession with horses and carriages suggest pleasures of this life continued in the afterlife. Both side door frames have scenes of female dancers and a pair of horses and carriages. On the doors with their images of large mask and ring handles are glimpses of a heavenly paradise represented by mythic creatures including auspicious red birds.

ROM ARTIFACTS

The collection of Chinese art in the Royal Ontario Museum is one of the most comprehensive and diversified outside China. Some of the best known and most informative objects from more than 35,000 artifacts in the collection are now on display in the Joey and Toby Tanenbaum Gallery of China, spanning more than 10,000 years of Chinese history. Most objects in the following pages have been selected from this gallery, giving additional examples of art produced during the periods represented in the exhibition.

This pictorial *hu* wine vessel, with scenes including an archery competition, banquet, prize giving, and a land and water battle, is similar in decoration to the vessel exhibited (see page 30). Bronze with copper inlay. Warring States period (481–221 BC) Ht. 33 Di. 22 cm Dr. Herman Herzog Levy Bequest Fund

Fu Food Vessel

Bronze   Western Zhou dynasty (1046–771 BC)   Le. 29.5 Ht. 22
Wi. 24.7 cm
Bishop William C. White Collection

The style and decoration of this vessel suggest that it was cast at about the same time as the *lai ding* with long inscription (see page 19). Like the ding, it was used for offering food to gods or ancestors. The inscription, cast on both the body and the lid, indicates it was commissioned by a marquis of the Chen state as part of a dowry gift to a relative.

Alliances between states and powerful families were common during Western Zhou, as China was broken up into numerous states and principalities of different sizes. The state of Chen was established by the Zhou royal family during this period, controlling territory in today's southeastern Henan province. In 568 BC, Chen became part of the powerful state of Chu in the south. Chu in turn was conquered by the state of Qin in 223 BC, two years before the First Emperor's unification.

Chariot Fittings

Bronze; pole fittings with silver inlay   Warring States period (481–221 BC)
Le. 9.7 Di. 4.3 cm; Le. 8.8 Di. 4.3 cm (pole fittings) Le. 18.7 Wi. 3
Dp. 7.9 cm; Le. 19.2 Wi. 3 Dp. 8.1 cm (crossbow rests)
Bishop William C. White Collection

These chariot fittings were among objects that came into the ROM collection in the 1920s and 1930s. Their exact function was unknown before the discovery in 1978 of a half-sized bronze chariot and covered carriage near the First Emperor's tomb mound. Those unique bronze vehicles are now permanently installed in China and thus do not travel.

Use of horse-drawn vehicles is known from the Shang dynasty onward, appearing in China about 1200 BC. As they were made almost entirely of perishable materials like wood and leather, only the bronze fittings have survived. The First Emperor's bronze vehicles reveal that the ROM fittings at the bottom formed a pair attached to the front of a chariot to support a crossbow. The others (top) were part of a coupling device that slipped over the pole of the vehicle's parasol. These decorative fittings reportedly came from royal tombs of Eastern Zhou kings near Luoyang.

Pendant

Jade   Spring and Autumn period (771–481 BC)   Le. 3.6 Wi. 3.6
Thickness 0.5 cm
Gift of Sir Robert Mond

This beautifully carved piece from a pendant set is a type commonly seen among jade ornaments from the Qin state. Shaped like a vertical bow knot, it has decoration on one face only; the other side remains plain. It is pierced at top and bottom by three evenly spaced perforations running at an angle through to the back. The decoration is divided into three zones; in the centre are a few incised horizontal lines; above and below them, the stone is pierced by symmetrically placed lines, the spaces between them filled with a fine incised geometric design.

Jade ornaments were a valuable part of aristocratic costume during Zhou times. The exhibition contains a number of jade pendants that were recovered from burials of Qin dukes or nobles (see page 23). This ROM jade pendant was likely worn by a nobleman (or noblewoman) of the Qin state.

Ridge Tile

Earthenware   Warring States period (481–221 BC)   Le. 90 Ht. 20
Wi. 30 cm
The George Crofts Collection

This very large roof ridge title was used on a grand royal palace in the state of Yan, one of the six powerful rival states finally conquered by Qin before unification. Similar tiles have been discovered from sites within the First Emperor's tomb complex.

Trying to halt Qin's chain of victories, the state of Yan planned to kill the King of Qin, the future First Emperor. In 227 BC, an assassin was sent by Yan's crown prince from their capital Xiadu (where the ROM tile was collected) to Xianyang to meet the King of Qin. There he feigned submission by his state and approached the king. As a famous stone relief of the 2nd century AD shows, he failed in his mission when his dagger hit a column instead of the king. The king is shown walking away unscathed, wearing a long sword similar to one shown in the exhibition.

Tiger Tally

Bronze   Qin dynasty (221–206 BC)   Le. 15 cm
Sir Edmund Walker Collection

According to early texts, tallies in the form of tigers were used by rulers during the Warring States period for issuing commands to mobilize the army. This bronze tiger tally came into the ROM collection in 1918, before any actual examples had yet been excavated in China. In 1973, the first archaeological find of bronze tiger tallies was unearthed near Xi'an, with inscriptions that verify their function. According to the inscriptions, a tiger tally had to be presented in order to mobilize any force of more than 50 persons. The ROM tiger tally, like those excavated, has two halves; one half was given to a general in the field, the other half stayed with the emperor. When the emperor sent a command, he had a courier bring his half to the general. If the two halves fitted, the general knew the order really came from the emperor.

Model of a Pigpen

Green-glazed earthenware   Han dynasty (206 BC–AD 220)   Ht. 16
Wi. 15.8 Dp. 16 cm
The George Crofts Collection

In ancient China it was believed that after death the "spirit-soul" travelled to the land of the immortals, and individual existence continued with all the necessities and luxuries provided that had been used in life. The First Emperor's faith in an afterlife is exemplified by his elaborate tomb structures and lavish burial goods, including the terracotta soldiers and many other objects in the exhibition.

The belief that motivated the First Emperor in planning his tomb complex persisted into the Han dynasty, though on a more modest scale, and the emphasis shifted from warfare to agriculture and food production. Models of domestic animals, entertainers, workers, and buildings tell us a great deal about life at the time. This model typically shows a pigpen below the privy with its tile roof.

Lamp

Bronze   Western Han dynasty (220 BC–AD 24)   Ht. 43.3 cm
Dr. Herman Herzog Levy Bequest Fund

Lamps were common household utensils and are frequently found at Han dynasty archaeological sites. One of the bronze lamps in the exhibition was used in the famous Changle palace in the Han capital Chang'an, just north of modern Xi'an. The ROM lamp is in the form of a long-necked bird, possibly a wild goose, similar to some of the bronze birds found in Pit K0007 in the First Emperor's pleasure park. The bird stands on the back of a tortoise, which represents the direction of north in Han cosmology. Its wings and tail feathers are indicated with fine recessed lines. The lamp consists of five parts: the body of the bird; its neck and head holding the lid in its beak; a small, handled tray for burning oil; and adjustable lampshades. The openwork grille on one of the shades shows two entwined four-footed dragons.

Director's Signature Series
The Warrior Emperor and China's Terracotta Army

TUESDAY, MAY 18

Motel to Mogul: Isadore Sharp

Isadore Sharp is the Founder, Chairman, and Chief Executive Officer of Four Seasons Hotels and Resorts. He built his first hotel in 1961. Four Seasons operates 83 hotels in 35 countries.

An Evening with Deepak Chopra begins at 7 p.m. and takes place at Convocation Hall, 31 King's College Circle, University of Toronto.

Price: Ground Floor an d Rise Area $63, 1st Balcony $42, 2nd Balcony $26.25.

VIP tickets on the Ground Floor with a special reception where Deepak Chopra will be present, $150. All tickets for this event are only available at: www.uofttix.ca or call 416·978·8849.

TUESDAY, JUNE 15

On Being a Celebrity in China: Mark Rowswell

Since his first appearance on Chinese television in 1988, Mark Rowswell has been an extremely popular performer and on-air personality, and a cultural ambassador between China and the West.

WEDNESDAY, JUNE 23

An Evening with Deepak Chopra

Deepak Chopra has written more than 56 books translated into over 35 languages. He is a Fellow of the American College of Physicians and a member of the American Association of Clinical Endocrinologists.

THURSDAY, OCTOBER 14

The Man Who Loved China

Simon Winchester is a journalist, broadcaster, and bestselling author of 20 books, including the current *New York Times* bestseller *The Man Who Loved China*, the remarkable story of Joseph Needham.

The Warrior Emperor and China's Terracotta Army Lecture Series

THURSDAY, JUNE 24

Building Up and Digging Down: New Archaeological Evidence for the Construction of the Tomb Complex of the First Emperor

Dr. Chen Shen is the Bishop White Chair of East Asian Archaeology at the ROM, and is the senior curator who developed the exhibition *The Warrior Emperor and China's Terracotta Army*.

TUESDAY, JULY 6

Law and War in the Making of the Chinese Empire

Robin D. S. Yates, James McGill Professor of History and East Asian Studies, McGill University, is a specialist in Chinese history who focuses on science and technology, law, and women.

TUESDAY, SEPTEMBER 21

Newest Sources of Early Chinese History: Recently Discovered Inscribed Bronze Vessels

Edward L. Shaughnessy is the Lorraine J. and Herrlee G. Creel Distinguished Service Professor of Early China, Department of East Asian Languages and Civilizations, University of Chicago.

FRIDAY, SEPTEMBER 24

Before the Empire: New Light from Early Qin Archaeology

Li Feng is Associate Professor of Early Chinese History and Archaeology, Department of East Asian Languages and Cultures, Columbia University, and an expert in ancient Chinese bronzes and bronze inscriptions.

The Warrior Emperor and China's Terracotta Army Lecture Series *Continued*

TUESDAY, SEPTEMBER 28

Art, War, and the Afterlife: What Survives the Great Cataclysms and Why?

Gary Geddes has written and edited more than 40 books and received 12 literary awards. His books *Swimming Ginger* and *The Terracotta Army* are steeped in Asian culture.

All lectures begin at 7 p.m. in the Signy and Cléophée Eaton Theatre at the ROM.

Price per lecture: $28, ROM Members and students $25. Choose any 4 lectures for $84, ROM Members and students $75. All 14 lectures: $252, ROM Members and students $225.

TUESDAY, OCTOBER 19

State Power and Sovereignty: The Success of the First Emperor

Dr. Roberto Ciarla is a specialist in Far Eastern prehistoric and proto-historic archaeology. He is the curator of the Far East section, National Museum of Oriental Art, Rome.

THURSDAY, OCTOBER 21

Visualizing the Underground World as Conceived by the First Emperor: Archaeological Implications

Dr. Duan Qingpo is Professor of Archaeology at Northwest University in Xi'an, and has been the chief archaeologist investigating the First Emperor's tomb complex during the past two decades.
This lecture is in Mandarin with English translation.

THURSDAY, OCTOBER 28

New Light on Xanadu

British historian John Man specializes in Mongolia and north China. His recent books include *The Terracotta Army*, *The Great Wall*, and *Xanadu: Marco Polo and Europe's Discovery of the East*.

THURSDAY, NOVEMBER 4

The Garden of Curious Things: Science and Technology in China at the Time of the Terracotta Warriors

Professor Rick Guisso has taught the history of premodern China in the Department of East Asian Studies, University of Toronto, for more than 30 years, serving two terms as Department Chair.

THURSDAY, NOVEMBER 11

Use and Abuse: The Qin Dynasty in Later Histories

Professor Michael Nylan is the author of seven books about Confucian Classics and the archaeology and history of the classical era, two translations, and 50 articles.

WEDNESDAY, NOVEMBER 17

China's Ancient Green Revolution

Archaeologist Gary Crawford, a Fellow of the Royal Society of Canada and member of the Department of Anthropology, University of Toronto, specializes in environmental issues and the origins of agriculture.

THURSDAY, NOVEMBER 25

From Terracotta Army to Jade Suits: A Golden Age in Chinese History

Carol Michaelson, a curator of Chinese art at the British Museum, is also curating an upcoming exhibition of Qin and Han material at the Museum of Far Eastern Antiquities, Stockholm.

THURSDAY, DECEMBER 2

Battle for an Empire

Dr. Graham Sanders is an Associate Professor, Department of East Asian Studies, University of Toronto. His most recent book, *Words Well Put*, examines poetry as a persuasive form of discourse.

THURSDAY, DECEMBER 9

Writing Fiction About China as a Foreigner

Former theatre director David Rotenberg is now Artistic Director of The Professional Actors Lab. His writing includes the Zhong Fong mystery novels, *Shanghai*, and *The Ivory Compact*.

Royal Ontario Museum
100 Queen's Park
Toronto, Ontario M5S 2C6
www.rom.on.ca

Library and Archives Canada Cataloguing in Publication

Shen, Chen, 1964–
      The warrior emperor and China's terracotta army / Chen Shen.

Published to accompany the exhibition of the same name opened at the Royal Ontario Museum in June 2010. Also published in French under the title: L'empereur guerrier de Chine et son armée de terre cuite. Includes bibliographical references.

ISBN 978-0-88854-478-0
    1. Qin shi huang, Emperor of China, 259–210 B.C.—Tomb—Exhibitions.
    2. Terra-cotta sculpture, Chinese—Qin-Han dynasties, 221 B.C.–220 A.D.—
    Exhibitions. 3. Excavations (Archaeology)—China—Shaanxi Sheng—
    Exhibitions. 4. Shaanxi Sheng (China)—Antiquities—Exhibitions. 5. Royal
    Ontario Museum—Exhibitions. I. Royal Ontario Museum II. Title.
DS747.9.Q254S43 2010   931'.04   C2010-902722-1

Managing Editor: Glen Ellis; Research Editor: Barbara Stephen; Copy Editor: Caroline Kaiser; Designer: Tara Winterhalt

Cover photo: Infantry Soldier, Earthenware 221–206 BC, Ht. 189 cm, Emperor Qin Shihuang's Terracotta Army Museum

Photography courtesy the Shaanxi Cultural Heritage Promotion Centre with the following exceptions—pages 4–5, 9, 11, 12, 14, 17, 40: Brian Boyle, ROM; page 58 (top): Science Press Beijing. Care has been taken to trace the ownership of any copyright material contained in this text. The publishers welcome any information that will enable them to rectify, in subsequent editions, any incorrect or omitted reference or credit.

Printed and bound in Canada by Transcontinental Interglobe, Beauceville East, Quebec

The Royal Ontario Museum is an agency of the Government of Ontario.

Mixed Sources

Product group from well-managed forests, controlled sources and recycled wood or fiber
www.fsc.org Cert no. SW-COC-000952
©1996 Forest Stewardship Council

FSC